Grab Another Partner!

Twelve Tremendous Partner Songs for Young Singers

Arranged, with new words and music,

by Sally K. Albrecht and Jay Althouse

Includes Reproducible Student Song Sheets and Staging Suggestions

See back cover for CD Track Numbers.   * staging suggestions included

©MMIII by Alfred Publishing Co., Inc.
All Rights Reserved. Printed in USA.
Cover illustration by Charles Grace
Photography by Scott Moody

Alfred

ISBN 0-7390-3039-6 (Book)
ISBN 0-7390-3040-X (CD)
ISBN 0-7390-3041-8 (Book/CD Kit)

About the Composers

SALLY K. ALBRECHT

Sally K. Albrecht is the Director of School Choral Publications for Alfred Publishing. She is a popular choral conductor, composer, and clinician, especially known for her work with choral movement. Sally is the author of two books on the subject, **Choral Music in Motion, Volumes 1 and 2**, and also has produced many choral movement videos, distributed by Alfred.

An annual recipient of the ASCAP Special Music Award since 1987, Sally has over 200 popular choral publication in print, as well as many larger elementary songbooks, musicals, programs, and cantatas. She also compiled and edited **The Choral Warm-Up Collection**, featuring 167 choral warm-ups contributed by 51 choral music educators.

A native of Cleveland, Ohio, Sally received a B.A. Degree from Rollins College with a double major in Music and Theater. From there she moved to the University of Miami, where she received both an M.A. in Drama and an M. M. in Accompanying. She has worked with literally thousands of teachers and students through festivals, conventions, and workshops in over 40 states, Canada, Singapore, and Australia.

JAY ALTHOUSE

Jay Althouse received a B.S. degree in Music Education and a M.Ed degree in music from Indiana University of Pennsylvania. For eight years he served as a rights and licenses administrator for a major educational music publisher. During that time he served a term on the Executive Board of the Music Publishers Association of America.

As a composer of choral music, Jay has over 500 works in print for choirs of all levels. He is a writer member of ASCAP and is a regular recipient of the ASCAP Special Award for his compositions in the area of standard music.

His book, **Copyright, The Complete Guide for Music Educators, 2nd Edition**, is recognized as the definitive sourcebook on the subject of copyright for music educators. Jay has also co-written several songbooks, musicals, and cantatas with his wife, Sally K. Albrecht, and has compiled and arranged a number of highly regarded vocal solo collections. He is the co-writer of the best-selling book, **The Complete Choral Warm-Up Book**, published by Alfred. Most recently, he co-authored **Accent on Composers**, a reproducible sourcebook for classroom music teachers featuring the music and lives of 22 composers

ABOUT THE RECORDING

Grab a Partner! tracks were recorded at October Genius Studio - Bluffton, SC
Vocal recording and mixing were done at Red Rock Recording - Saylorsburg, PA

Darryl E. Horne - *Instrumental Arranger, MIDI Tracks*
Sally K. Albrecht - *Keyboard, Producer*
Jennifer Butz, Janice Lee, Danielle Molan, Danielle Snyder, and Ashley Taylor - *Vocals*

in case you missed it...

GRAB A PARTNER!
Twelve Terrific Partner Songs for Young Singers

Arranged, with new words and music,
by Sally K. Albrecht and Jay Althouse

20172 Teacher's Handbook

20173 SoundTrax CD

20174 CD KIT: Book/CD

www.alfred.com

Visit the Alfred Website for more information on these
and other Alfred elementary materials.

1. COME BACK, LIZA
(Watah Come a Me Eye)

Arranged, with new
words and music, by
SALLY K. ALBRECHT
and **JAY ALTHOUSE**

Jamaican Folk Song

* Water comes to my eyes - I cry!

21677

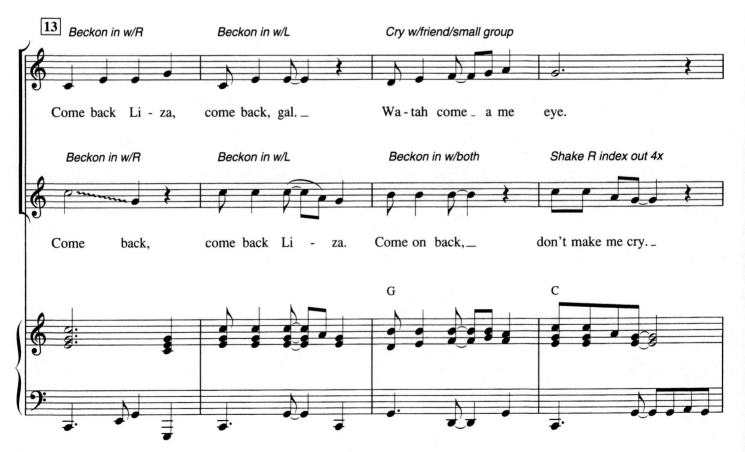

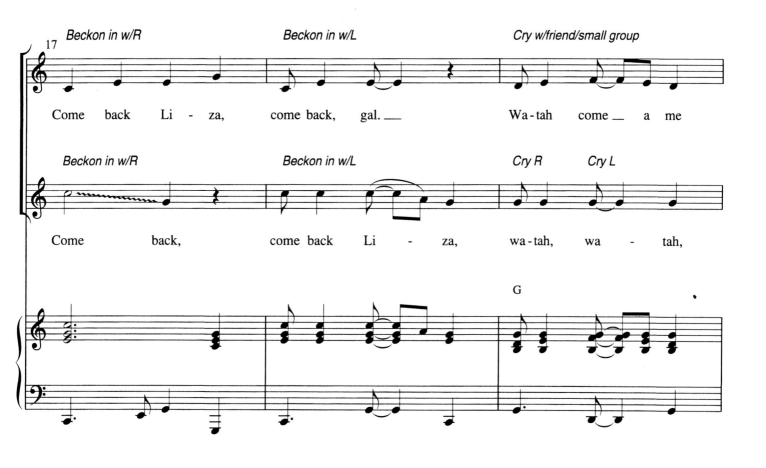

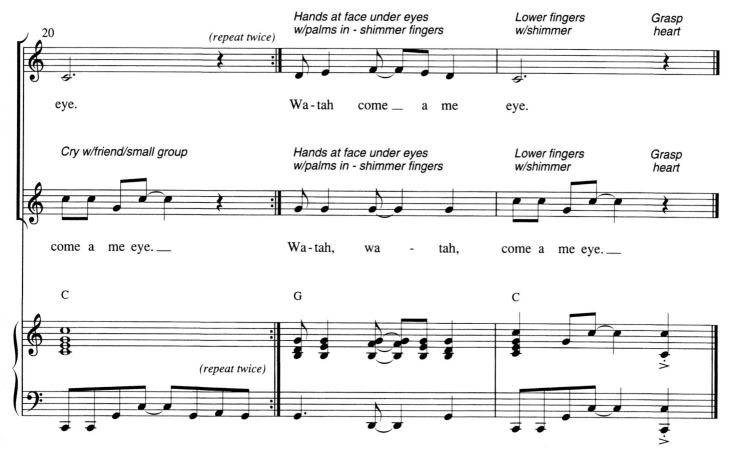

2. SLEEP, BABY, SLEEP

(Schlaf, Kindlein, Schlaf)

Arranged, with new
words and music, by
SALLY K. ALBRECHT

German Folk Song

PRONUNCIATION GUIDE

Schlaf, Kind-lein, schlaf,
Schlahf, Kint-line, schlahf,

Der Vat - er hüt't die schaf,
Dehr Fah-tehr hyt' t* dee schahf,

Die Mut - ter schut-telt's Baü-me - lein,
Dee Moo-tehr schoot-tehlz Boy-meh-line,

Da fällt her - ab ein träu-me - lein.
Dah fehlt hare-ahb ine troy-meh-line.

Schlaf, Kind-lein, schlaf.
Schlahf, Kint-line, schlahf.

* Hüt't – no English equivalent, say an "oh" with the lips, but the tongue is raised in the back of the mouth as if saying "eh."

3. WINTER SLEIGH RIDE
(Over the River and Through the Wood)

*Arranged, with new
words and music, by*
SALLY K. ALBRECHT
and **JAY ALTHOUSE**

Traditional

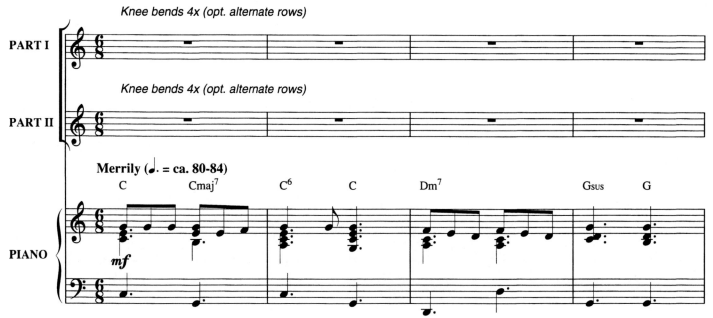

21677

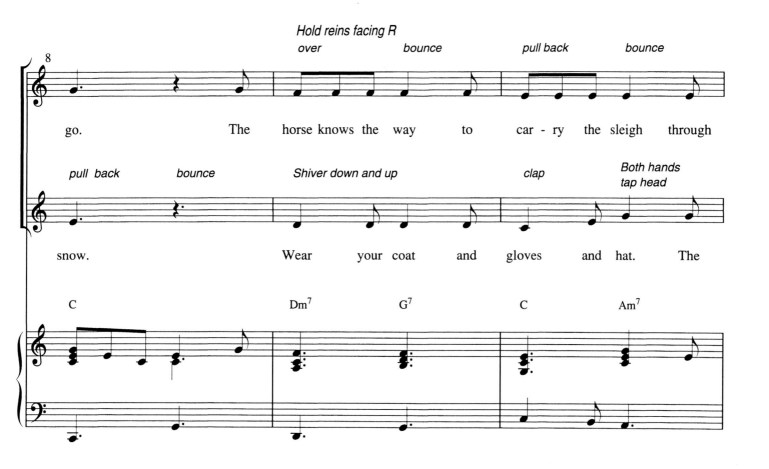

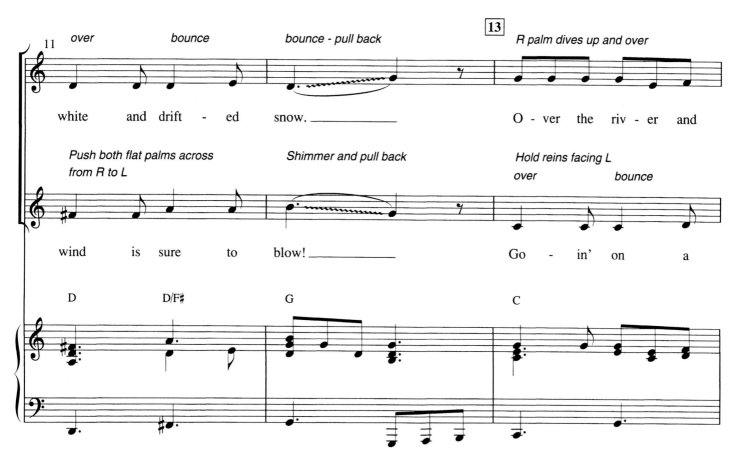

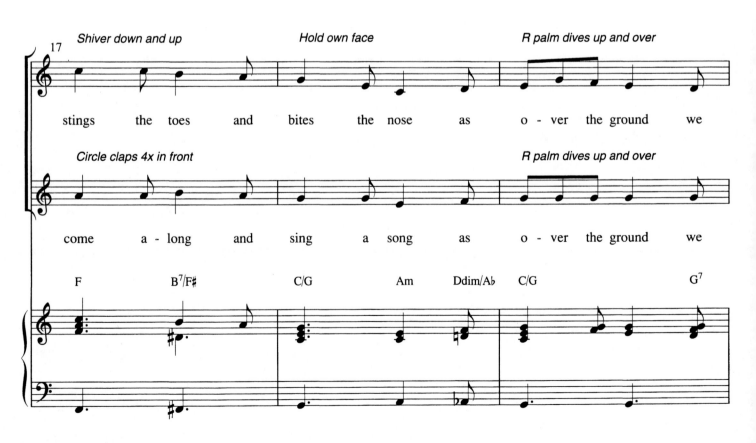

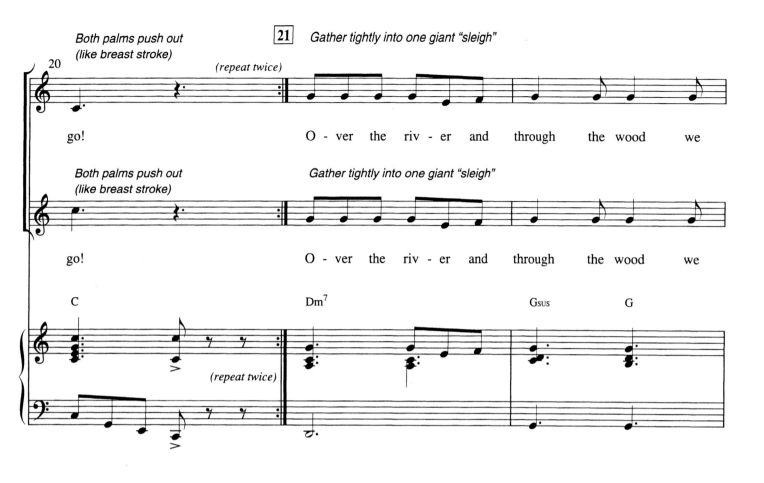

4. TO JOY
(Beethoven's Ode to Joy)

Arranged, with new
words and music, by
SALLY K. ALBRECHT
and **JAY ALTHOUSE**

Music by
LUDWIG VAN BEETHOVEN

5. PEACE
(Shalom Chaverim)

Arranged, with new
words and music, by
SALLY K. ALBRECHT

Israeli Folk Song

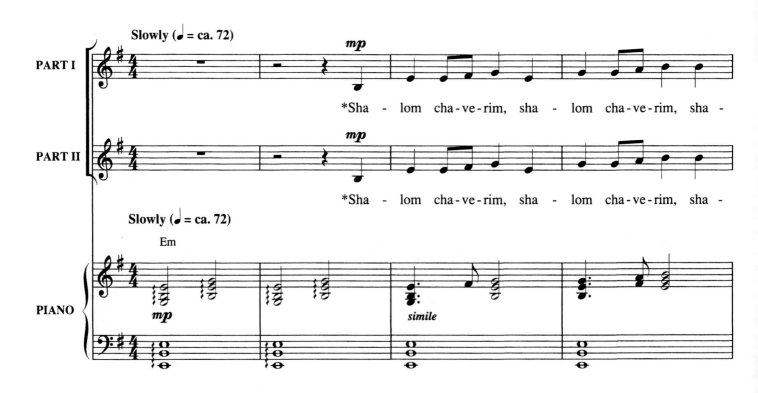

* Shah-lohm chah-veh-reem, Leh-heet-rah-oht. (Goodbye/peace, good friends, etc.)

6. RIDE THE SWEET CHARIOT!

(Swing Low, Sweet Chariot/Ride the Chariot)

Arranged, with new
words and music, by
SALLY K. ALBRECHT

Traditional Spirituals

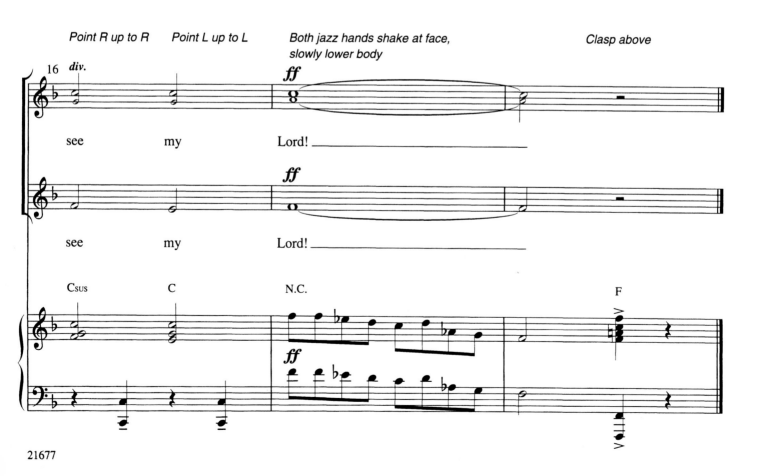

7. JINGLE ALL THE WAY!

(Jingle Bells)

Arranged, with new
words and music, by
SALLY K. ALBRECHT

by **JAMES PIERPONT**

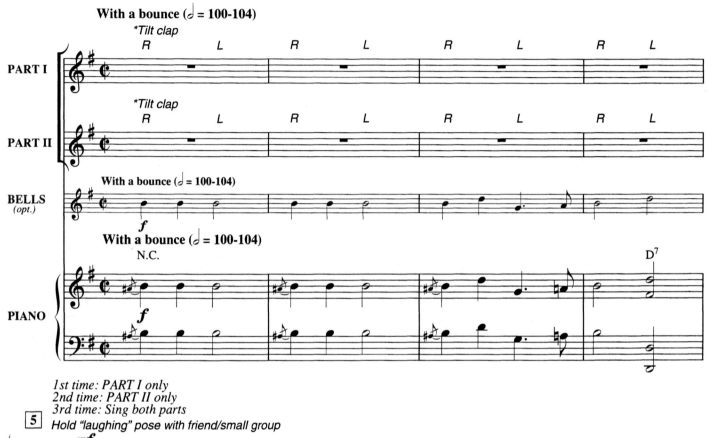

1st time: PART I only
2nd time: PART II only
3rd time: Sing both parts

Hold "laughing" pose with friend/small group

* Tilt clap - Arms look like windshield wipers, clap from side to side, palms facing each other.
  Opt: for this song, several students may wear wrist bells.

21677

8. PHONE TAG
(Hello, My Baby)

Arranged, with new
words and music, by
SALLY K. ALBRECHT
and **JAY ALTHOUSE**

by **JOE HOWARD**
and **IDA EMERSON**

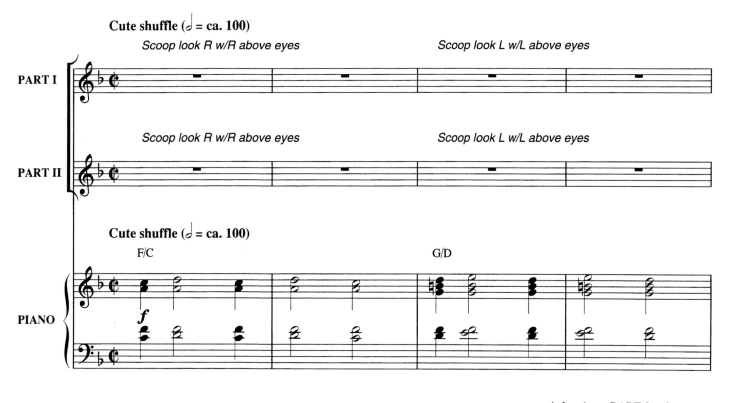

* *1st time: PART I only*
2nd time: PART II only
3rd time: Sing both parts

* NOTE: Director may use only guys on PART I and gals on PART II. Change the lyric (guy/gal) as needed.
  All singers should have telephone receiver in pocket (or small toy phone/cell phone).
  OR select only one singer in each part to have phone. Others react around him/her.

21677

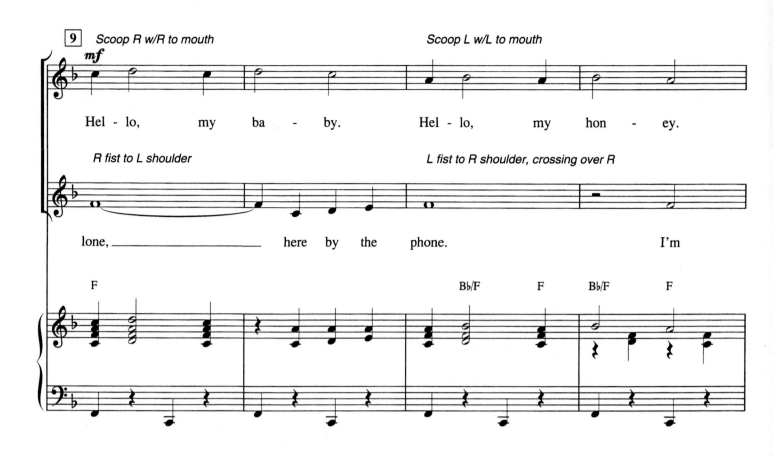

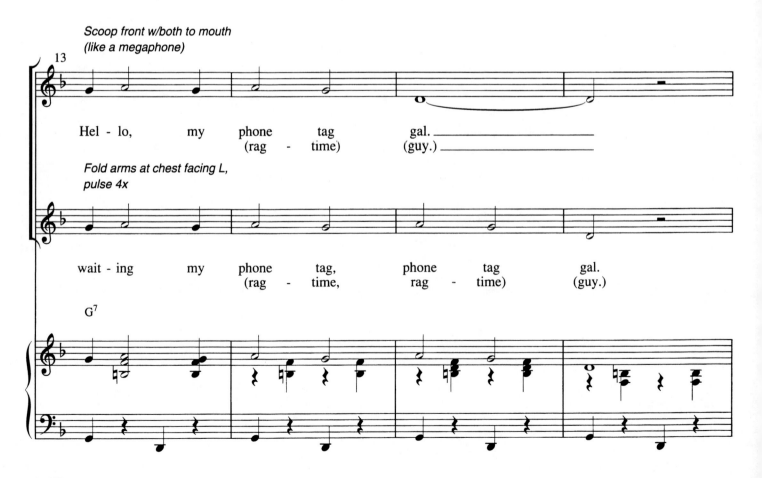

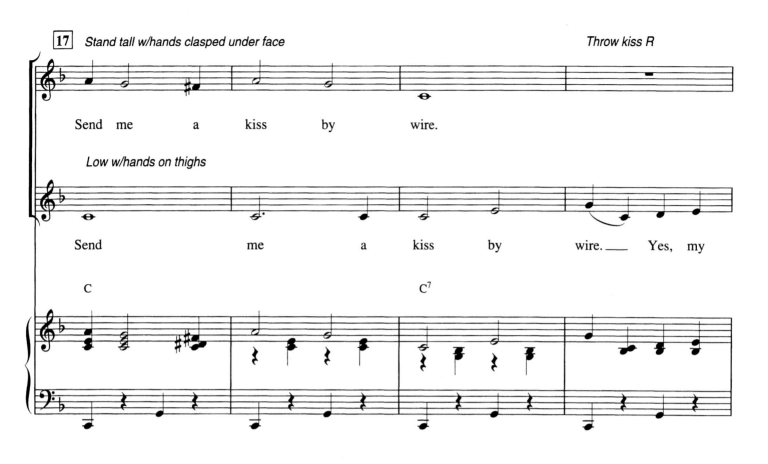

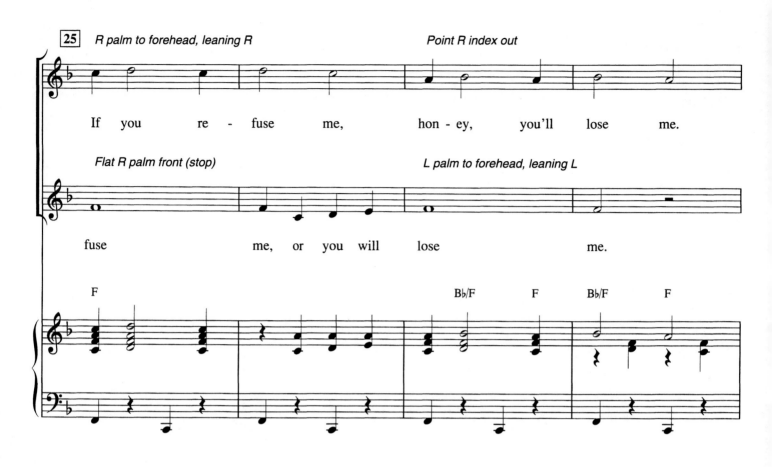

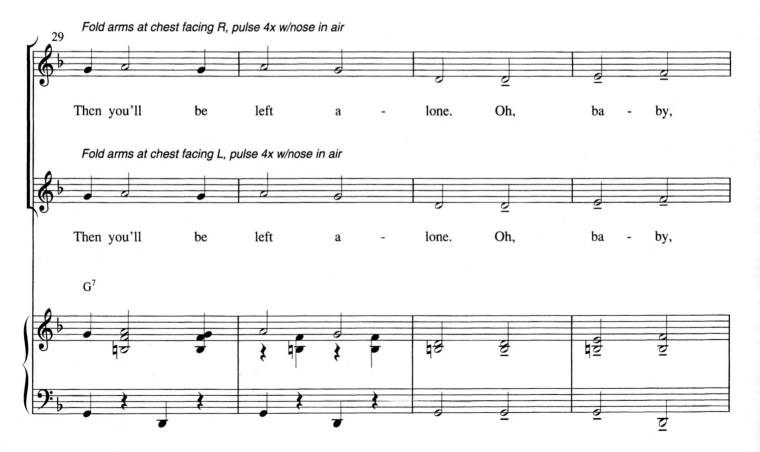

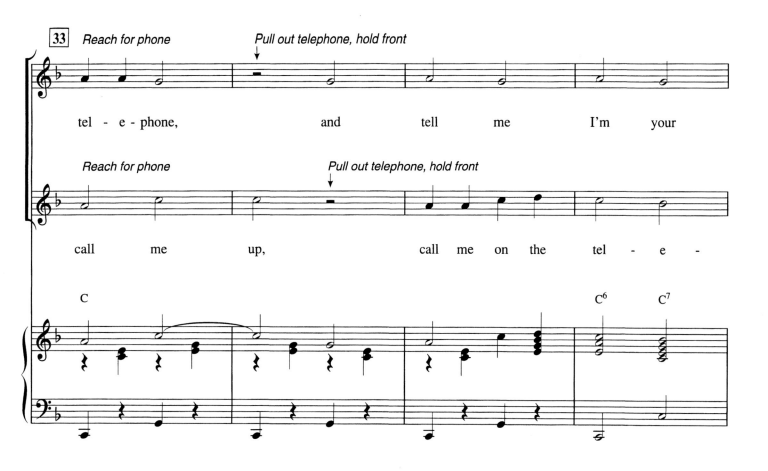

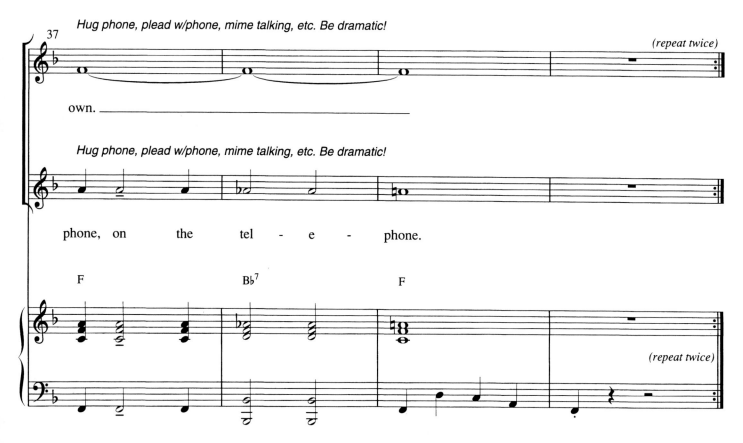

9. SIT DOWN!
(Sit Down, Servant/ Oh, Won't You Sit Down)

Arranged, with new
words and music, by
SALLY K. ALBRECHT

Traditional Spirituals

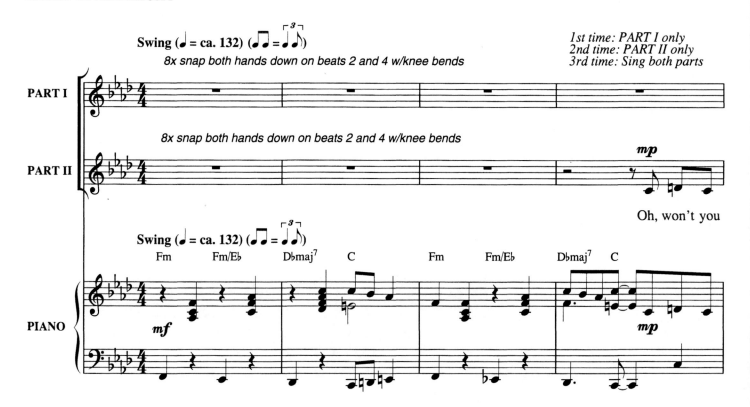

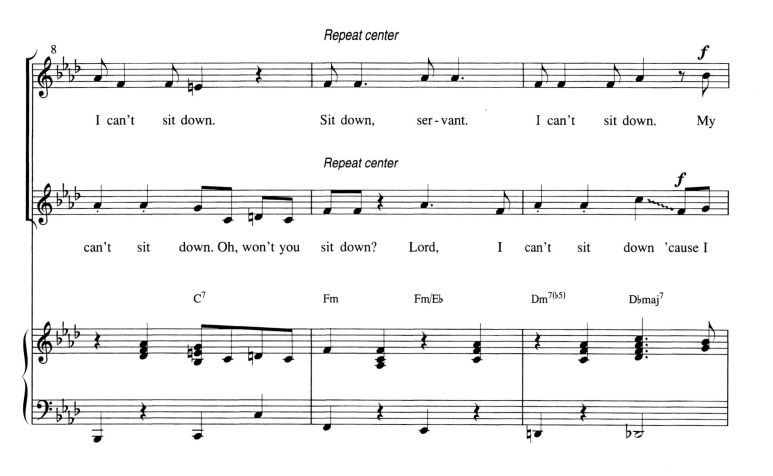

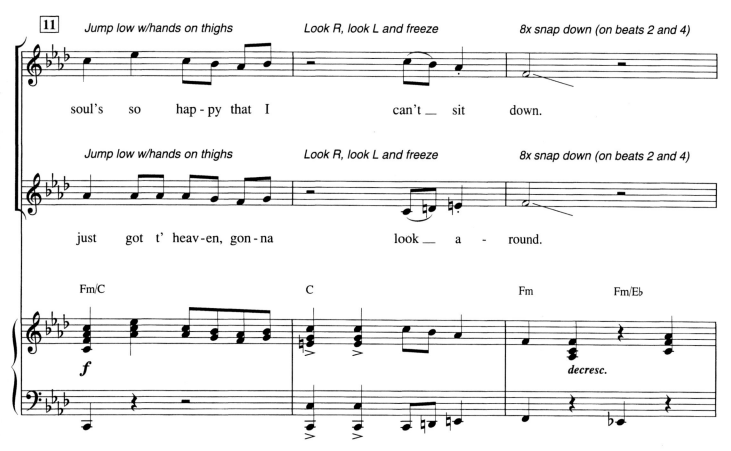

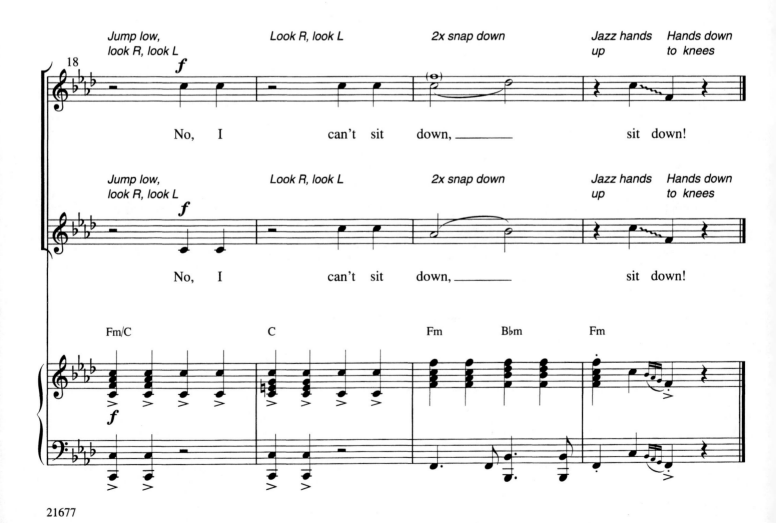

10. HIGH FLYING FLAG
(You're A Grand Old Flag)

Arranged, with new
words and music, by
SALLY K. ALBRECHT
and **JAY ALTHOUSE**

by GEORGE M. COHAN

1st time: PART I only
2nd time: PART II only
3rd time: Sing both parts

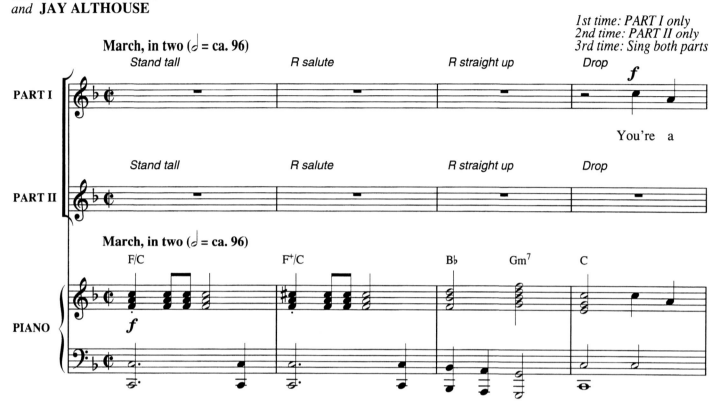

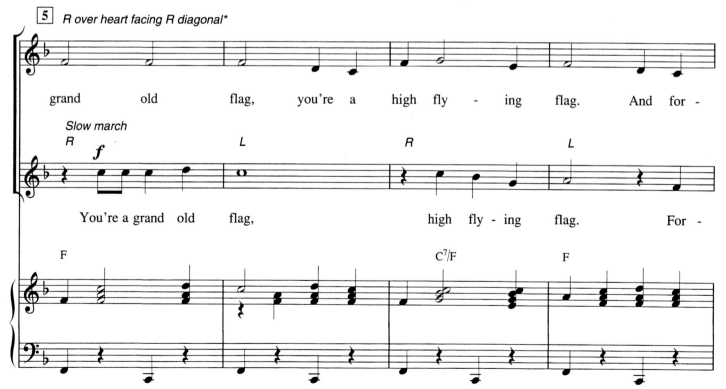

* An American flag may be placed stage R.

21677

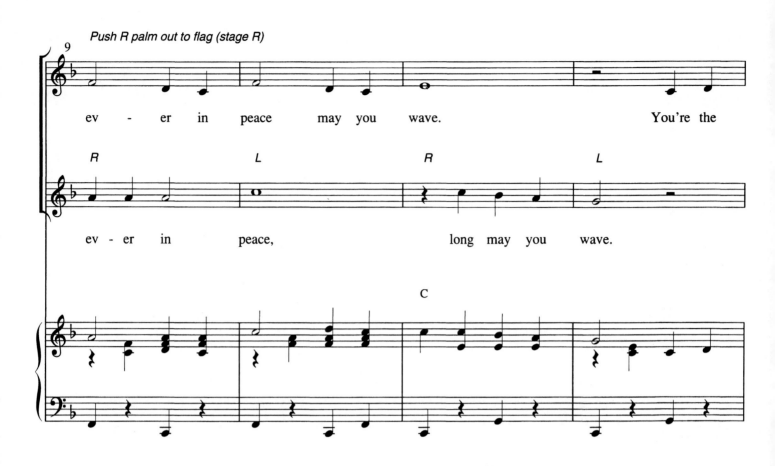

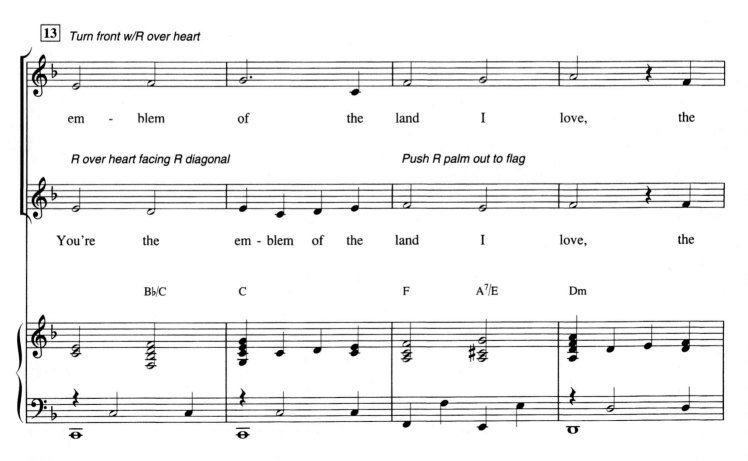

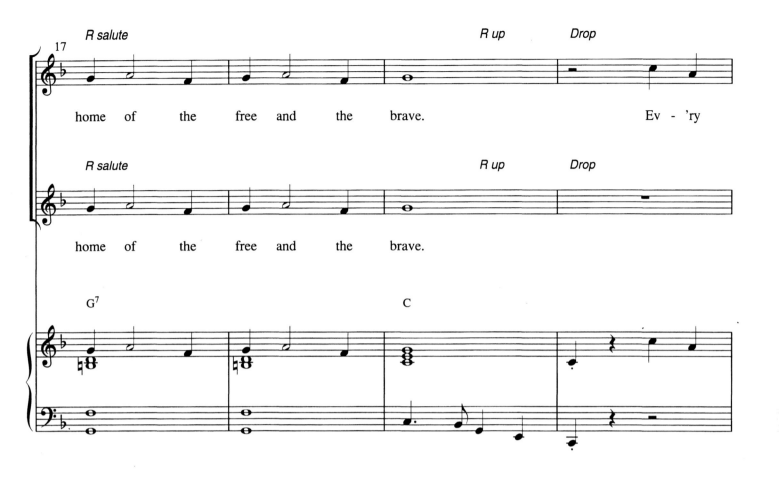

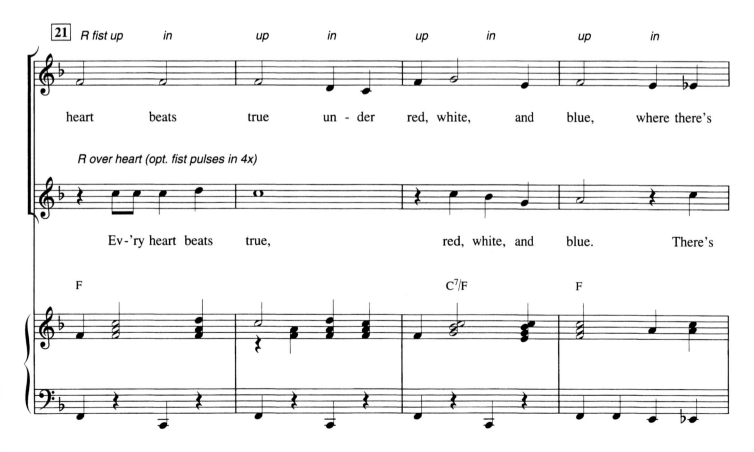

21677

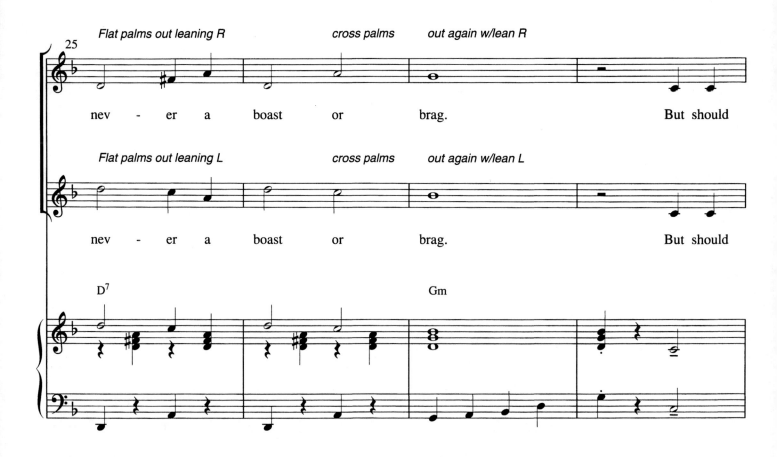

nev - er a boast or brag. But should

nev - er a boast or brag. But should

29 *Scoop into clusters*

auld ac - quain - tance be for - got. Keep your

auld ac - quain - tance be for - got.

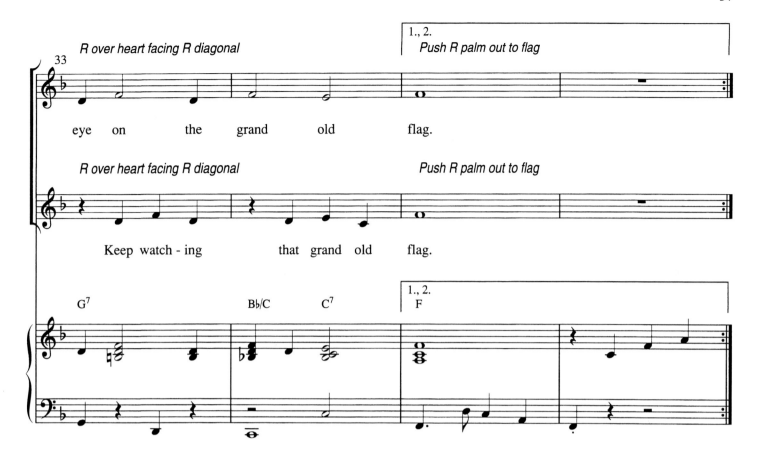

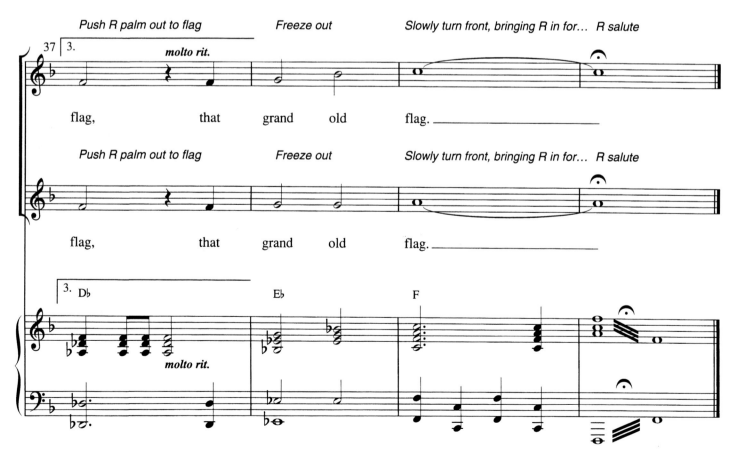

11. SIERRA LOVE SONG
(Cielito Lindo)

*Arranged, with new
words and music, by*
SALLY K. ALBRECHT
and **JAY ALTHOUSE**

Mexican Folk Song

*1st time: PART I only
2nd time: PART II only
3rd time: Sing both parts*

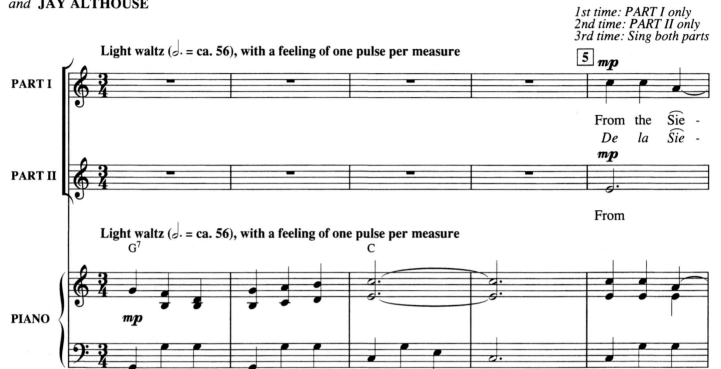

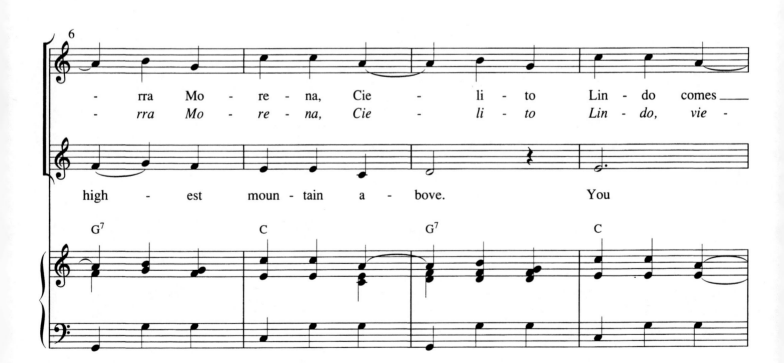

25

Sing,   now,   no   cry - ing. _____   Be -
Can - ta y   no   llo - res, _____   por -

Do   not   cry   if   we   must   part.

Dm   G⁷   F/G   C

29

cause when your ___ voice is ring - ing, Cie - li - to   Lin - do,   my ___
que can - tan _ do se a - le - gran, Cie - li - to   Lin - do,   los ___

Ay,   Ay,   ay,   ay. _____   For

G⁷   Dm

34   1., 2.   3.

__ heart is sigh - ing.   sigh - ing.
__ co - ra - zo - nes.   zo - nes.

you have my heart.   heart.

G⁷   1., 2.
          C   3.
                       C

Pronunciation Guide and Translation of CEILITO LINDO

De la Sie - rra Mo - re - na, Cie - li - to Lin - do, vie - nen ba - h a n - d o.

Deh lah See͡eh-rah Moh-reh-nah, See͡eh-lee-toh Leen-doh, vee͡eh-nehn bah-hahn-doh.

(From the Sierra Morena, Cielito Lindo comes down.)

Un par de͡o - ji - tos ne - gros Cie - li - to Lin-do de con - tra-b a n - d o.

Oohn pahr deh͡oh-hee-tohs neh-grohs See͡eh-lee-toh leen-doh deh kohn-trah-bahn-doh.

(A pair of black eyes, Cielito Lindo, her jewels.)

Ay, ay, ay, ay! Can - ta͡y no llo - res,

Ah-ee, yiee, yiee, yiee! Kan-tah͡ee noh yoh-rehs.

(Ay! Sing, and don't cry.)

Por - que can - tan - do se͡a - le-gran, Cie - li- to Lin-do, los co - ra - zo - nes.

Pohr-keh kahn-tahn-doh seh͡ah-leh-gran, See͡eh-lee-toh Leen-doh, lohs kor-rah-zoh-nehs.

(Because singing makes hearts happy, Cielito Lindo.)

12. COME HEAR THE BAND!

(Alexander's Ragtime Band)

Arranged, with new
words and music, by
SALLY K. ALBRECHT
and **JAY ALTHOUSE**

by **IRVING BERLIN**

1st time: PART I only
2nd time: PART II only
3rd time: Sing both parts

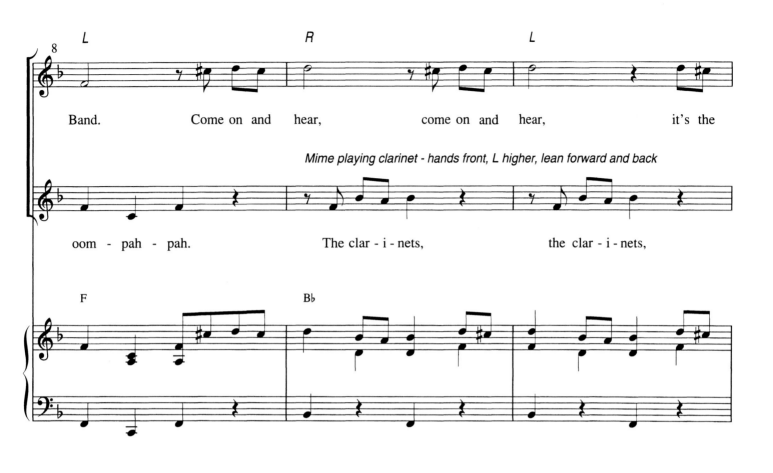

Band.   Come on and hear,   come on and hear,   it's the

Mime playing clarinet - hands front, L higher, lean forward and back

oom - pah - pah.   The clar - i - nets,   the clar - i - nets,

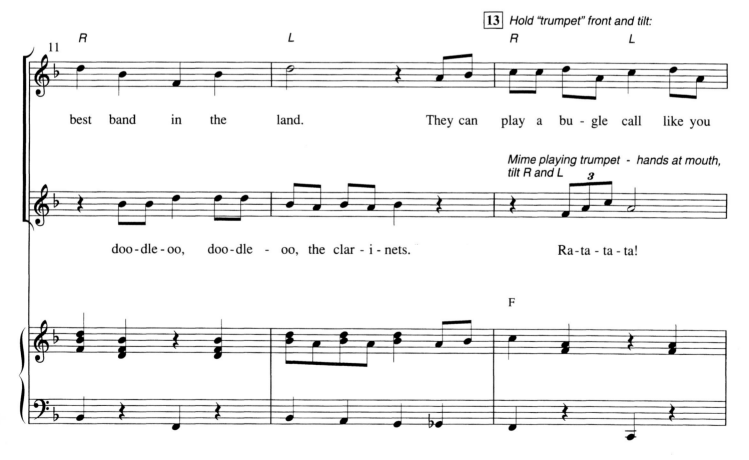

best   band   in   the   land.   They can   play a   bu - gle   call   like you

Mime playing trumpet - hands at mouth, tilt R and L

doo - dle - oo,   doo - dle - oo,   the   clar - i - nets.   Ra - ta - ta - ta!

13 *Hold "trumpet" front and tilt:*

44

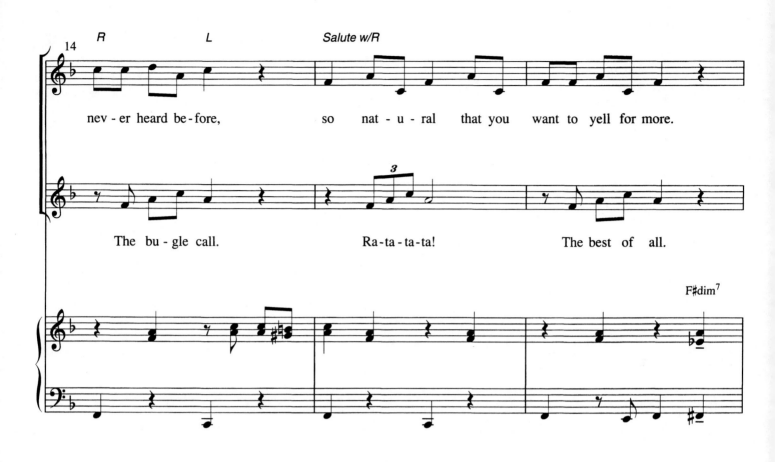

21677

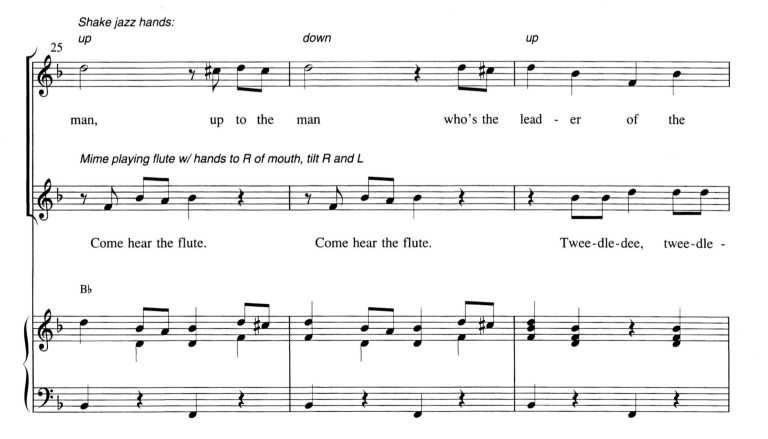

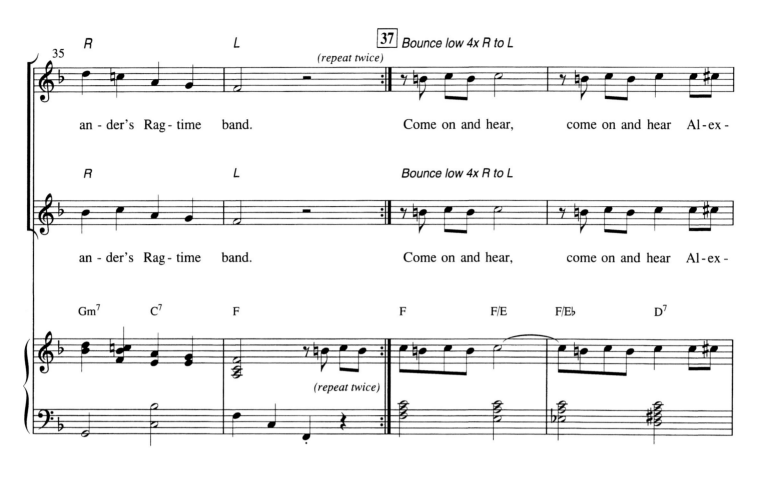

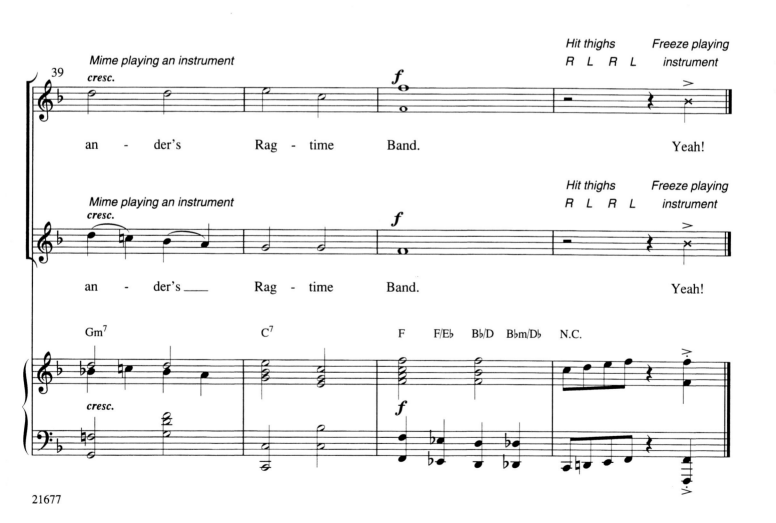

21677

Reproducible Student Pages

1. COME BACK, LIZA
(Watah Come a Me Eye)

*Arranged, with new
words and music, by*
SALLY K. ALBRECHT
and **JAY ALTHOUSE**

Jamaican Folk Song

*1st time: PART I only
2nd time: PART II only
3rd time: Sing both parts*

* Water comes to my eyes - I cry!

21677

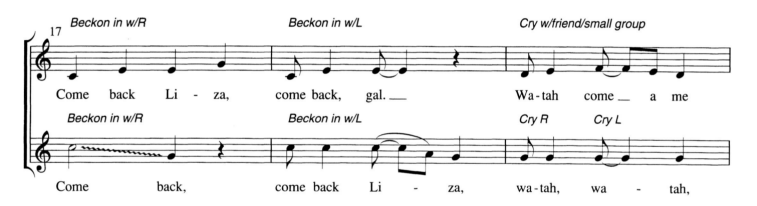

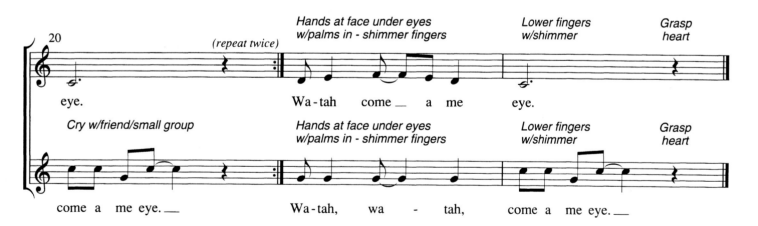

21677

2. SLEEP, BABY, SLEEP

(Schlaf, Kindlein, Schlaf)

Arranged, with new
words and music, by
SALLY K. ALBRECHT

German Folk Song

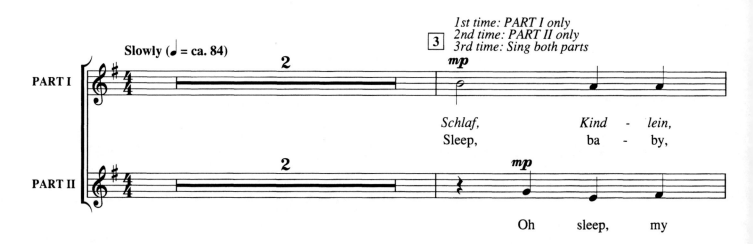

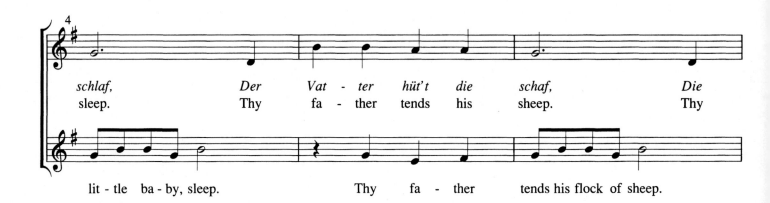

PRONUNCIATION GUIDE

Schlaf, Kind-lein, schlaf,
Schlahf, Kint-line, schlahf,

Der Vat - er hüt't die schaf,
Dehr Fah-tehr hyt't* dee schahf,

Die Mut - ter schut-telt's Baü-me - lein,
Dee Moo-tehr schoot-tehlz Boy-meh-line,

Da fällt her - ab ein träu-me - lein.
Dah fehlt hare-ahb ine troy-meh-line.

Schlaf, Kind-lein, schlaf.
Schlahf, Kint-line, schlahf.

* Hüt't – no English equivalent, say an "oh" with the lips, but the tongue is raised in the back of the mouth as if saying "eh."

21677

3. WINTER SLEIGH RIDE
(Over the River and Through the Wood)

Arranged, with new
words and music, by
SALLY K. ALBRECHT
and **JAY ALTHOUSE**

Traditional

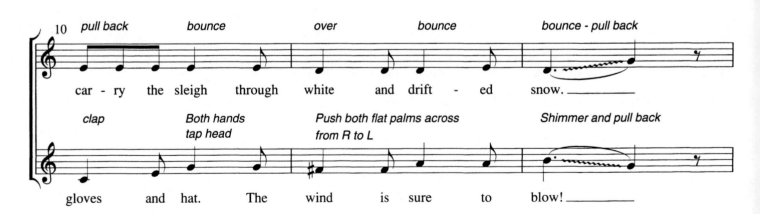

R palm dives up and over   Both palms push out (like breast stroke)   Both palms up over head R

O - ver the riv - er and through the wood. Oh, how the wind does

Hold reins facing L
over   bounce   pull back   bounce   Hands on thighs facing front, bounce low   bounce low

Go - in' on a sleigh ride. Read - y, set

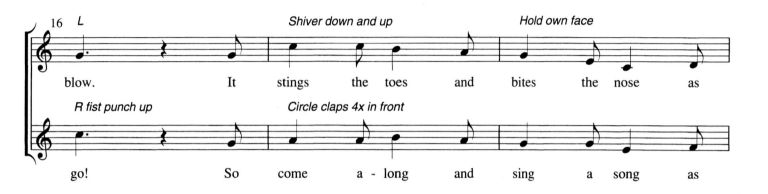

L   Shiver down and up   Hold own face

blow. It stings the toes and bites the nose as

R fist punch up   Circle claps 4x in front

go! So come a - long and sing a song as

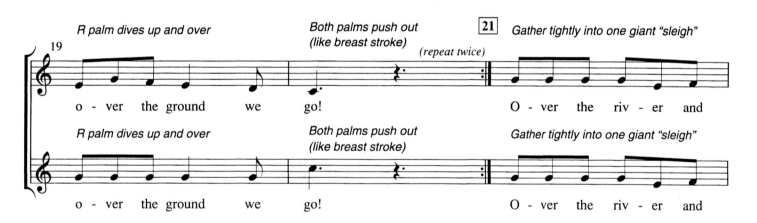

R palm dives up and over   Both palms push out (like breast stroke)   (repeat twice)   21   Gather tightly into one giant "sleigh"

o - ver the ground we go!   O - ver the riv - er and

R palm dives up and over   Both palms push out (like breast stroke)   Gather tightly into one giant "sleigh"

o - ver the ground we go!   O - ver the riv - er and

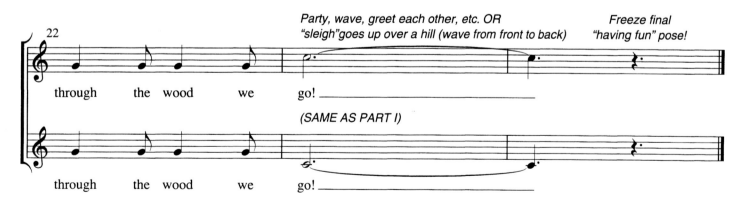

Party, wave, greet each other, etc. OR "sleigh" goes up over a hill (wave from front to back)   Freeze final "having fun" pose!

through the wood we go! _____

(SAME AS PART I)

through the wood we go! _____

4. TO JOY
(Beethoven's Ode to Joy)

Arranged, with new
words and music, by
SALLY K. ALBRECHT
and **JAY ALTHOUSE**

Music by
LUDWIG VAN BEETHOVEN

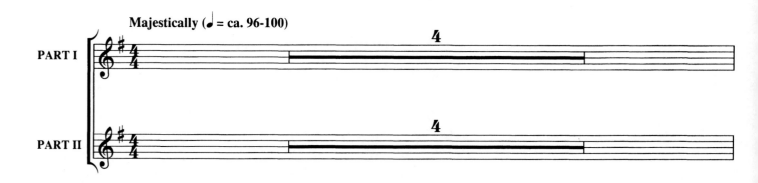

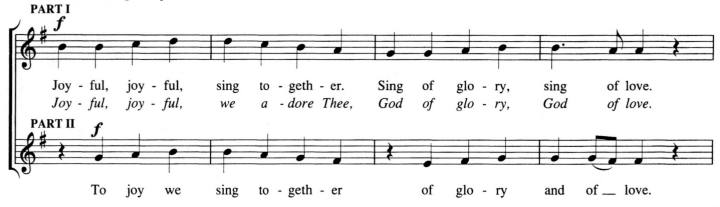

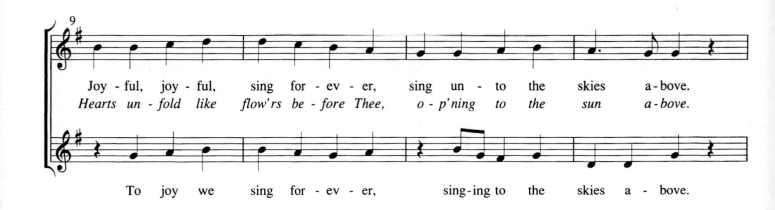

13

Melt the clouds of fear and _ sad - ness. Drive the _ dark of doubt a - way.

sin

Joy! Joy! Sing joy! Drive all doubt _ a - way.

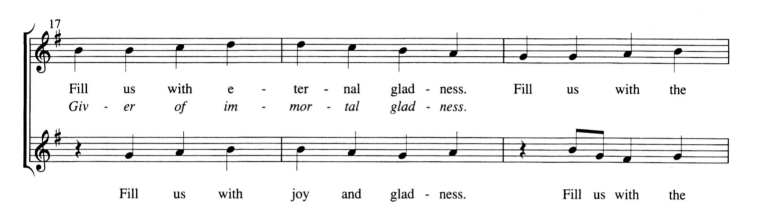

17

Fill us with e - ter - nal glad - ness. Fill us with the

Giv - er of im - mor - tal glad - ness.

Fill us with joy and glad - ness. Fill us with the

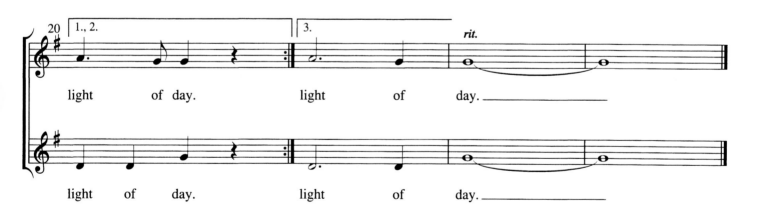

20 | 1., 2. | 3. | *rit.*

light of day. light of day. _____

light of day. light of day. _____

21677

5. PEACE
(Shalom Chaverim)

Arranged, with new
words and music, by
SALLY K. ALBRECHT

Israeli Folk Song

PART I
PART II

*Sha - lom cha-ve-rim, sha - lom cha-ve-rim, sha -

*Sha - lom cha-ve-rim, sha - lom cha-ve-rim, sha -

lom, sha - lom! L' - hit - ra - ot, l' - hit - ra - ot, sha -

lom, sha - lom! L' - hit - ra - ot, l' - hit - ra - ot, sha -

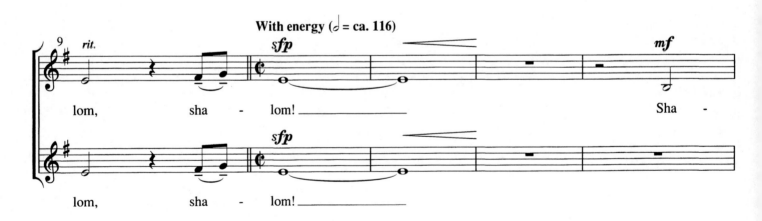

lom, sha - lom! _____ Sha -

lom, sha - lom! _____

* Shah-lohm chah-veh-reem, Leh-heet-rah-oht. (Goodbye/peace, good friends, etc.)

lom cha-ve-rim, sha-lom cha-ve-rim, sha-lom,

Sing a song of peace, oh, sing a song, my friend. Sha -

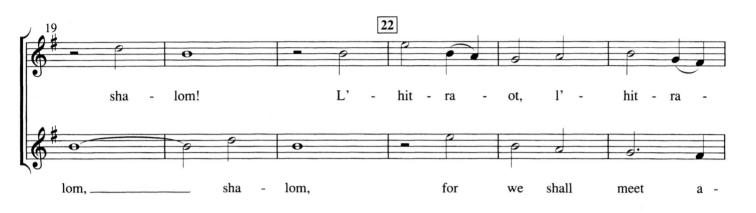

sha - lom! L' - hit-ra - ot, l' - hit-ra -

lom, _____ sha - lom, for we shall meet a -

ot, sha - lom, sha - lom! Sha - lom!

gain. Sha - lom, _____ sha - lom! ___ sha -

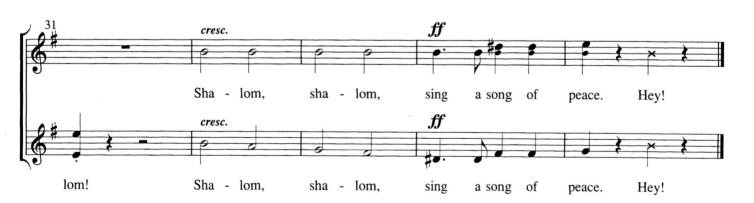

Sha - lom, sha - lom, sing a song of peace. Hey!

lom! Sha - lom, sha - lom, sing a song of peace. Hey!

21677

6. RIDE THE SWEET CHARIOT!
(Swing Low, Sweet Chariot/Ride the Chariot)

Arranged, with new
words and music, by
SALLY K. ALBRECHT

Traditional Spirituals

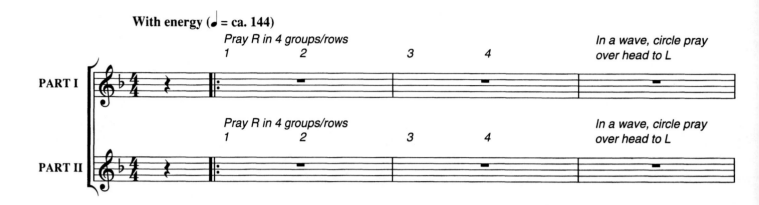

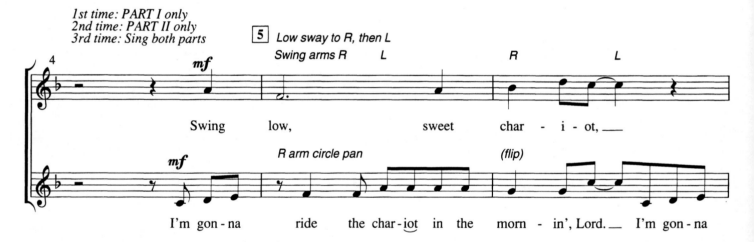

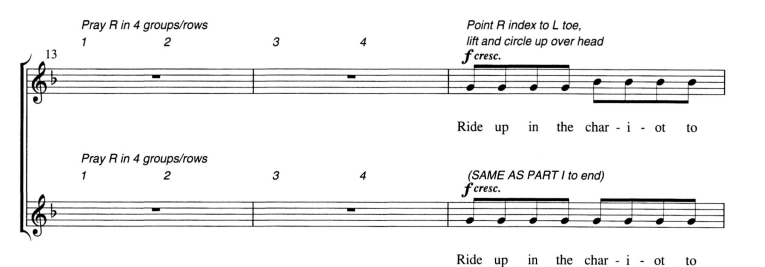

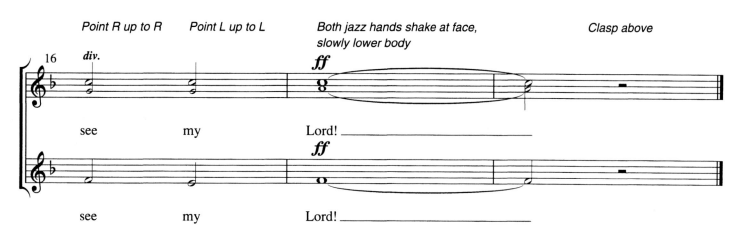

21677

7. JINGLE ALL THE WAY!

(Jingle Bells)

Arranged, with new words and music, by **SALLY K. ALBRECHT**

by **JAMES PIERPONT**

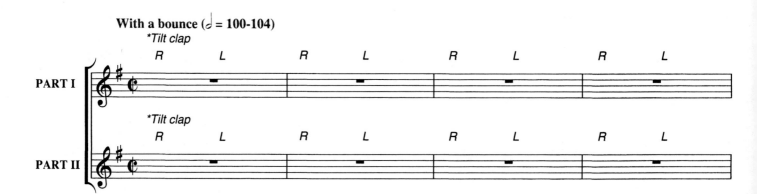

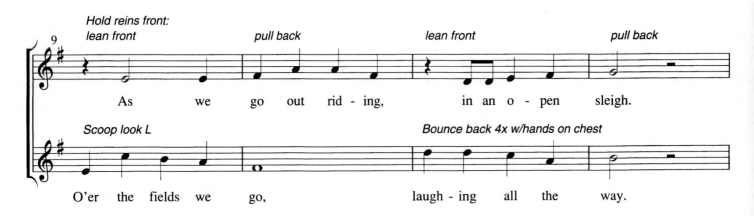

* Tilt clap - Arms look like windshield wipers, clap from side to side, palms facing each other.

Opt: for this song, several students may wear wrist bells.

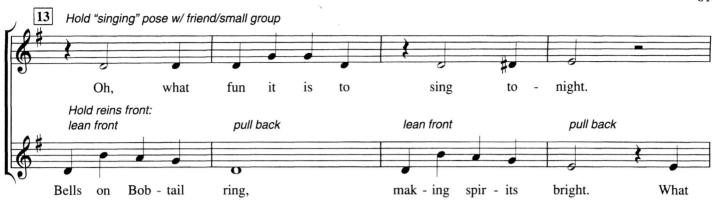

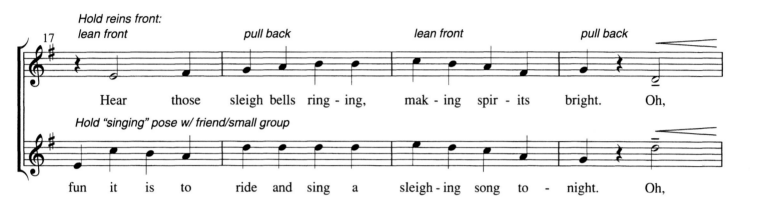

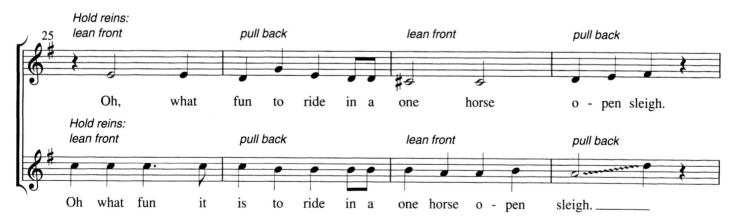

21677

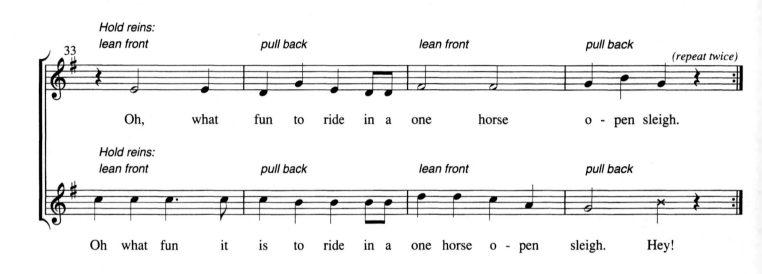

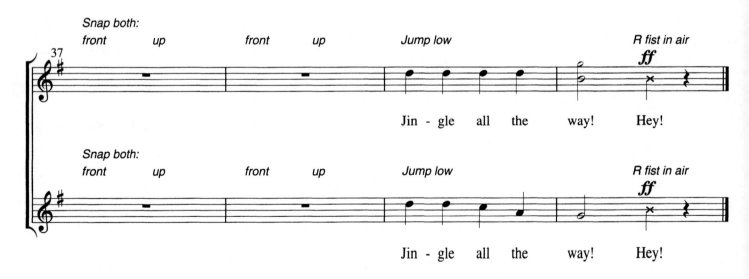

21677

8. PHONE TAG
(Hello, My Baby)

*Arranged, with new
words and music, by*
SALLY K. ALBRECHT
and **JAY ALTHOUSE**

by **JOE HOWARD**
and **IDA EMERSON**

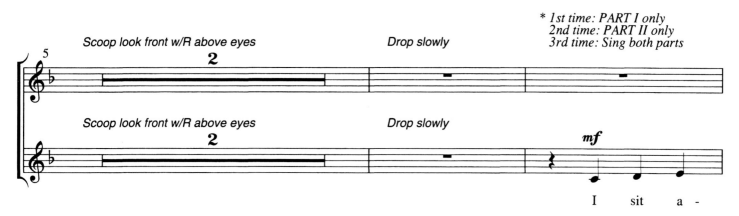

* NOTE: Director may use only guys on PART I and gals on PART II. Change the lyric (guy/gal) as needed.
All singers should have telephone receiver in pocket (or small toy phone/cell phone).
OR select only one singer in each part to have phone. Others react around him/her.

21677

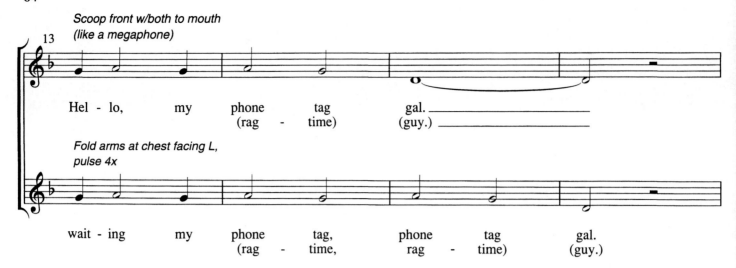

*Scoop front w/both to mouth
(like a megaphone)*

Hel - lo,   my   phone   tag   gal. _____
          (rag - time)   (guy.) _____

*Fold arms at chest facing L,
pulse 4x*

wait - ing   my   phone   tag,   phone   tag   gal.
          (rag - time,   rag - time)   (guy.)

17 *Stand tall w/hands clasped under face*   *Throw kiss R*

Send   me   a   kiss   by   wire.

Low w/hands on thighs

Send   me   a   kiss   by   wire. ___ Yes,   my

Both hands shimmer over heart   *Throw kiss L*

Ba - by,   my   heart's   on   fire.

Both hands shimmer over heart (stand tall)   *Clasp hands front, shake 3x low to high*
                                                        1   2   3

heart   is   on   fire. ___ Oh, please dar - ling don't re _

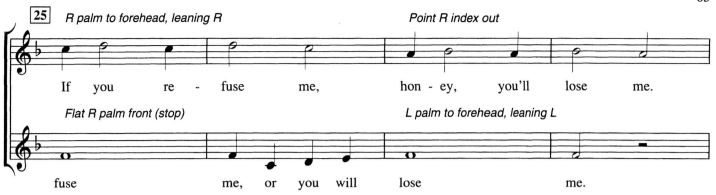

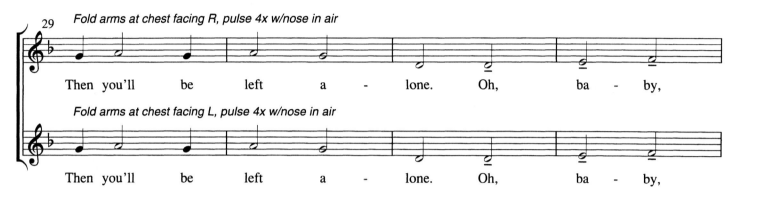

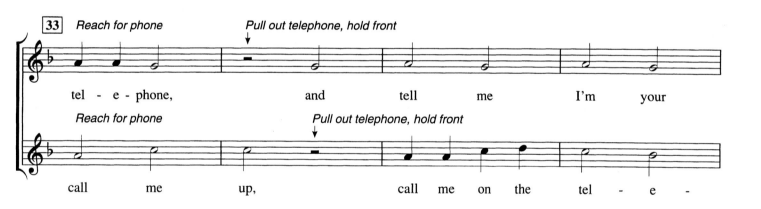

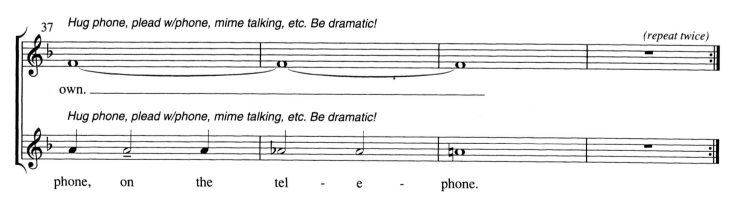

21677

9. SIT DOWN!
(Sit Down, Servant/ Oh, Won't You Sit Down)

Arranged, with new
words and music, by
SALLY K. ALBRECHT

Traditional Spirituals

1st time: PART I only
2nd time: PART II only
3rd time: Sing both parts

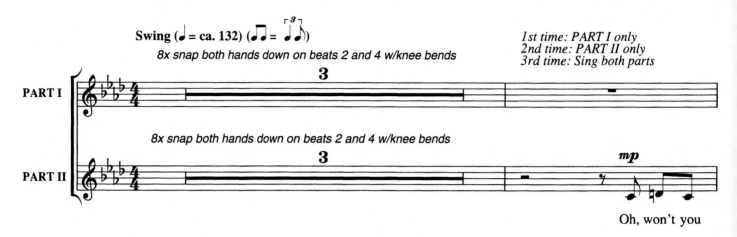

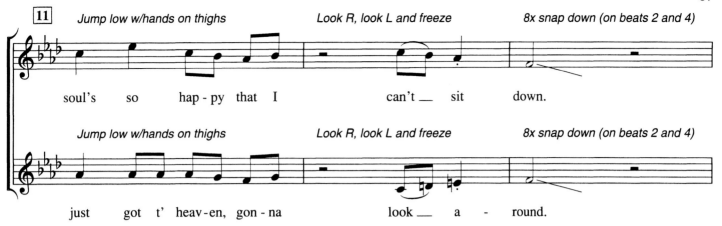

soul's so hap-py that I can't _ sit down.

just got t' heav-en, gon-na look _ a - round.

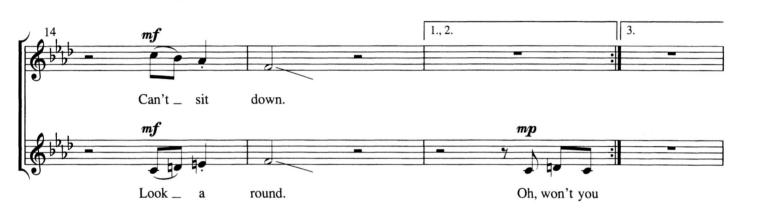

Can't _ sit down.

Look _ a round.

Oh, won't you

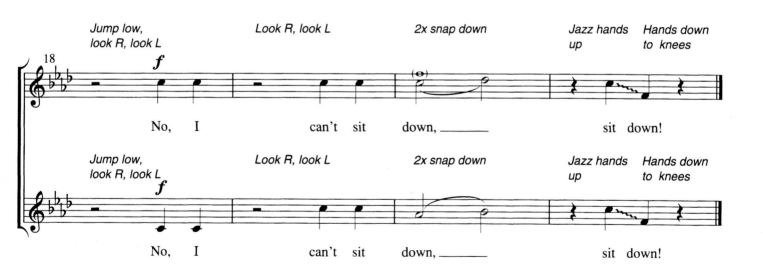

No, I can't sit down, _____ sit down!

No, I can't sit down, _____ sit down!

21677

10. HIGH FLYING FLAG
(You're A Grand Old Flag)

Arranged, with new
words and music, by
SALLY K. ALBRECHT
and **JAY ALTHOUSE**

by **GEORGE M. COHAN**

1st time: PART I only
2nd time: PART II only
3rd time: Sing both parts

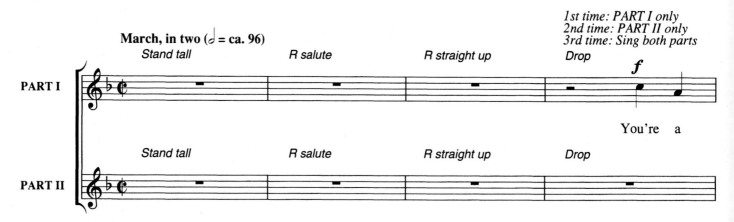

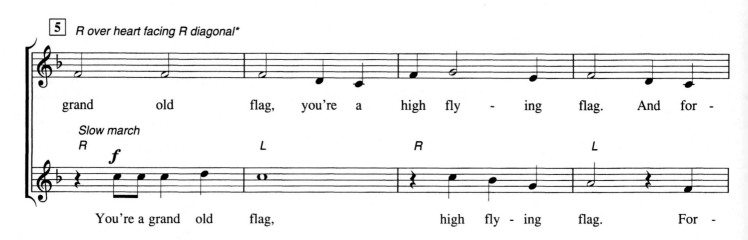

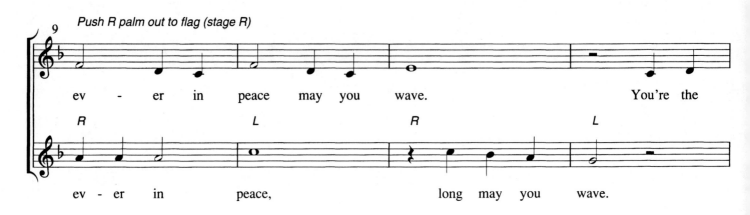

* An American flag may be placed stage R.

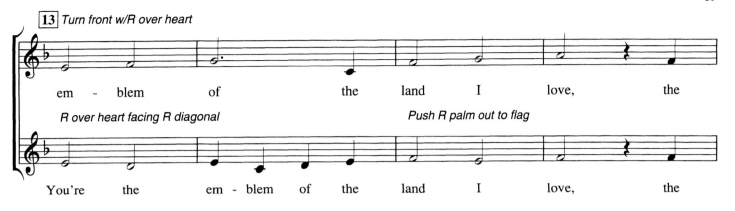

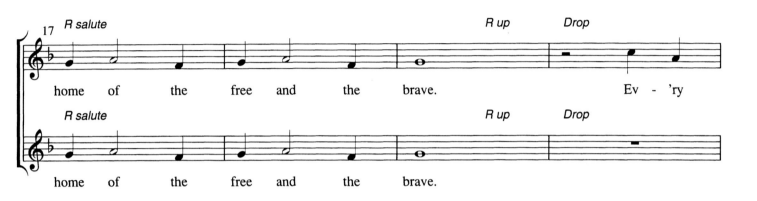

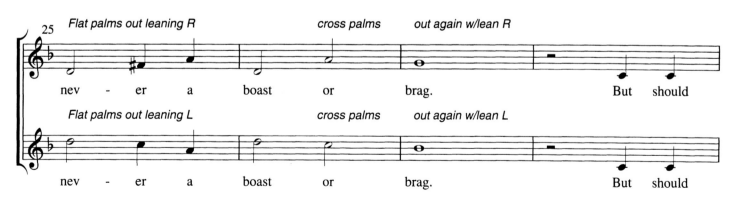

21677

29 *Scoop into clusters*

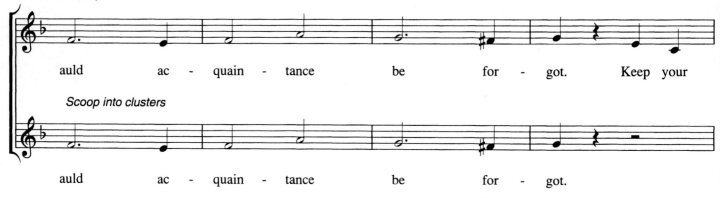

auld   ac - quain - tance   be   for - got.   Keep your

Scoop into clusters

auld   ac - quain - tance   be   for - got.

R over heart facing R diagonal

1., 2.
Push R palm out to flag

eye   on   the   grand   old   flag.

R over heart facing R diagonal   *Push R palm out to flag*

Keep   watch - ing   that   grand   old   flag.

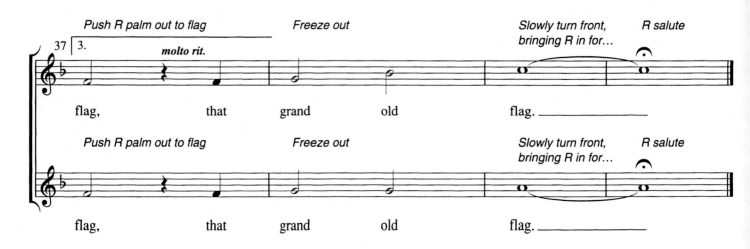

Push R palm out to flag   *Freeze out*   *Slowly turn front,*   *R salute*
bringing R in for...

3. *molto rit.*

flag,   that   grand   old   flag. _____

Push R palm out to flag   *Freeze out*   *Slowly turn front,*   *R salute*
bringing R in for...

flag,   that   grand   old   flag. _____

11. SIERRA LOVE SONG
(Cielito Lindo)

Arranged, with new words and music, by
SALLY K. ALBRECHT and JAY ALTHOUSE

Mexican Folk Song

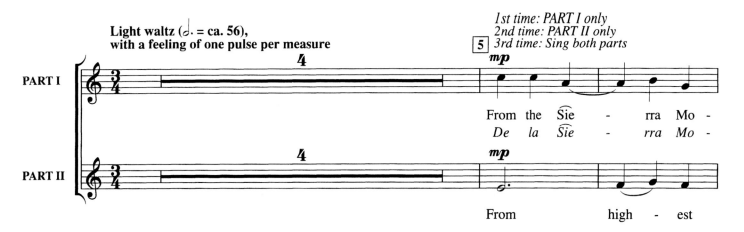

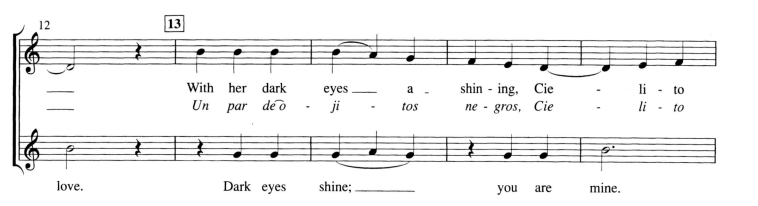

21677

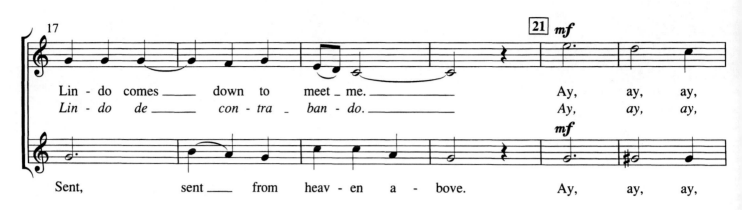

Lin - do comes ___ down to meet _ me. ___ Ay, ay, ay,
Lin - do de ___ con - tra _ ban - do. ___ *Ay, ay, ay,*

Sent, sent ___ from heav - en a - bove. Ay, ay, ay,

ay! ___ Sing, now, no cry - ing. ___ Be -
ay! ___ Can - ta y no llo - res, ___ por -

ay! ___ Do not cry if we must part.

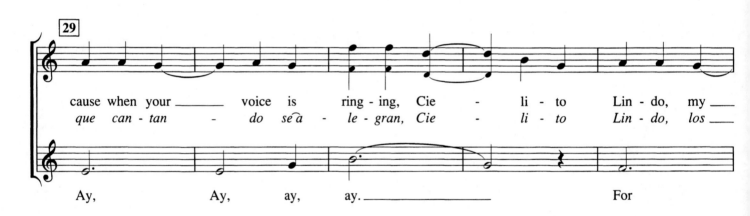

cause when your ___ voice is ring - ing, Cie - li - to Lin - do, my ___
que can - tan - do se a - le - gran, Cie - li - to Lin - do, los ___

Ay, Ay, ay, ay. ___ For

___ heart is sigh - ing. sigh - ing.
___ co - ra - zo - nes. zo - nes.

you have my heart. heart.

Pronunciation Guide and Translation of CEILITO LINDO

De la Sie - rra Mo - re - na, Cie - li - to Lin - do, vie - nen ba - han - do.

Deh lah See͡eh-rah Moh-reh-nah, See͡eh-lee-toh Leen-doh, vee͡eh-nehn bah-hahn-doh.

(From the Sierra Morena, Cielito Lindo comes down.)

Un par de͡o - ji - tos ne - gros Cie - li - to Lin-do de con - tra - ban - do.

Oohn pahr deh͡oh-hee-tohs neh-grohs See͡eh-lee-toh leen-doh deh kohn-trah-bahn-doh.

(A pair of black eyes, Cielito Lindo, her jewels.)

Ay, ay, ay, ay! Can - ta͡y no llo - res,

Ah-ee, yiee, yiee, yiee! Kan-tah͡ee noh yoh-rehs.

(Ay! Sing, and don't cry.)

Por - que can - tan - do se͡a - le-gran, Cie - li - to Lin-do, los co - ra - zo - nes.

Pohr-keh kahn-tahn-doh seh͡ah-leh-gran, See͡eh-lee-toh Leen-doh, lohs kor-rah-zoh-nehs.

(Because singing makes hearts happy, Cielito Lindo.)

12. COME HEAR THE BAND!
(Alexander's Ragtime Band)

Arranged, with new
words and music, by
SALLY K. ALBRECHT
and **JAY ALTHOUSE**

by **IRVING BERLIN**

1st time: PART I only
2nd time: PART II only
3rd time: Sing both parts

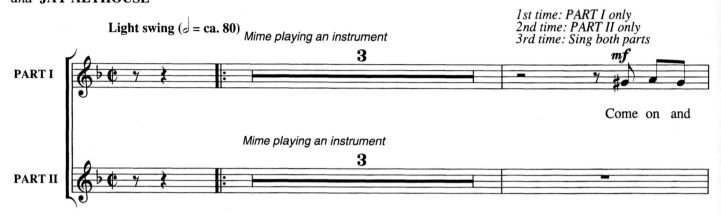

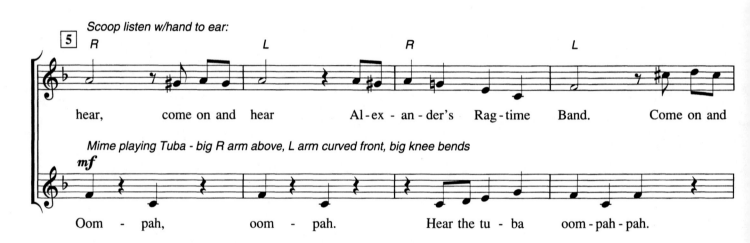

Copyright © MMIII by Alfred Publishing Co., Inc.
All Rights Reserved.   Printed in USA.

**NOTE: The purchase of this book carries with it the right to photocopy this page.
Limited to one school only. NOT FOR RESALE.**

21677

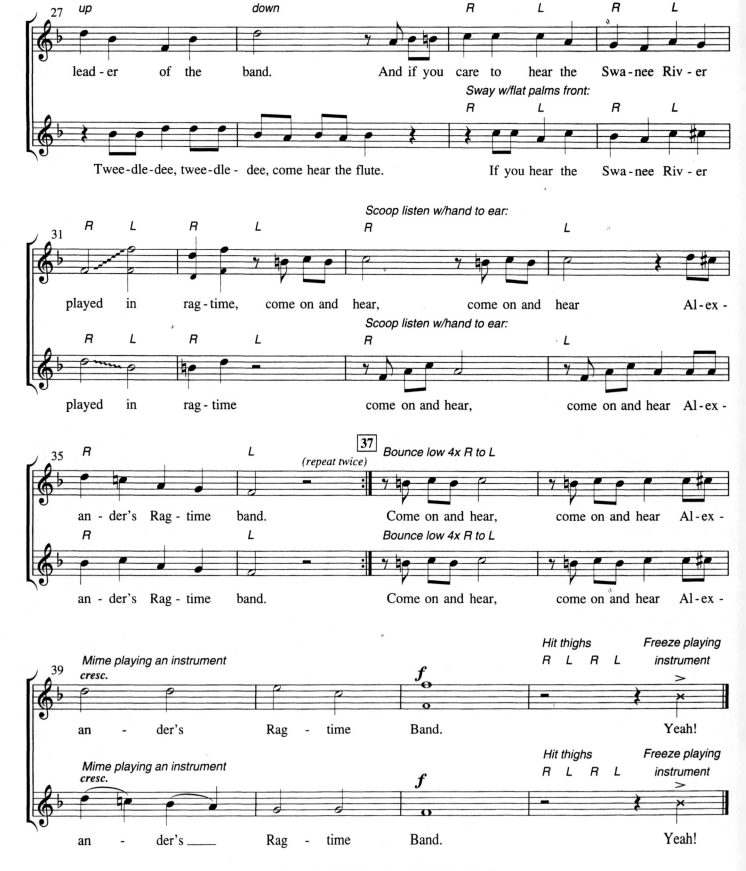

21677